Can't Stop the Rain

Heather Hammerstrom

Can't Stop the Rain © 2022 Heather Hammerstrom

All rights reserved.

No part of this publication may be reproduced, stored in a retrieval system, or transmitted, in any form or by any means, electronic, mechanical, photocopying, recording or otherwise, without the prior written permission of the presenters.

Heather Hammerstrom asserts the moral right to be identified as author of this work.

Presentation by *BookLeaf Publishing*

Web: www.bookleafpub.com

E-mail: info@bookleafpub.com

ISBN: 9789395413114

First edition 2022

DEDICATION

To the younger version of myself who still lives in the dark corners of my heart- I hope this gives you the voice you so desperately deserved.

Sweet Storm

The lumbering clouds of black puff
Stare down at me with convicting eyes
They gather together in a conspiracy huddle
Icily gazing at me

I hear the laughs of the teasing thunder from above
I feel the slap of the rain
Leaving my cold battered face bruised
With salty drops of my own eyes mixing

I let my soggy feet
Slop along the cracked sidewalk
Lazily trying to leave the storm behind

The trees around me sway slowly
As a bit of wind coaxes the bendable branches

The puddles that form around my slippery, soaked feet
Pull at my shoes like a whirlpool attack
I let the piles of glop
Grab at my soles
Until finally the gooey goblins succeed
And my shoes slip slowly off my feet

I barely notice my naked toes
As I keep my eyes fixed ahead

A gust of wind wisps through the air
And teases the threads of my coat
I outstretch my arms and
The jacket jauntily dances off my body
And into the sky somewhere

I lift my head to the heavens
And breathe in the smell of the storm

I laugh aloud into the clouds
And lick the droplets as they trickle onto my teeth
The clouds cock their heads
In amazement and delight
And slowly they trickle away
Leaving only a few lumbering droplets of mist
A crimson glow protrudes from the bits of leftover white

As my lungs expand
I allow the few bits of warm rays
To circulate through my body
Giving me an electric shock of life
I move my bare foot
So that it slams onto the cement
And all the cracks evaporate

At the sound of my step
And the puddles vanish
Each time my toes touch them

Complacency

I sit here knowing this is not where I want to be
Thoughts and feelings weighing heavy on me
Overwhelming sense of needing to escape
Yet fear incapacitating any step I would take
Heavy in my soul, an aching in my chest
For what I do not know- yet it offers me no rest
Waves that stay and never seem to wash away
Settled into the pit, those feelings just lay
I want to view myself as a lion, strong and brave
Yet always end up just feeling so naïve
With each day I live, I think I know less and less
Fading into the background, exasperating me I confess
More affected every day than I would ever let on
For when I do I feel the crumble of every one of my bonds
How do I navigate what they see and what I feel
Follow my own words and their success I might steal
Stuck on clichés of wisdom and prowess
When the reality of my ego is whittled down to much less
Words rattle in my brain with nowhere to go
In the end, it is all the same, complacency sows

Intersection

Day sets a murky tone on the swaying lanky stalks
The tall arms of dried yellow grass stand at attention
When the wind rouses
The stalks set off on a rustling marathon
The tips of the grain bow towards the black, car-driven tar
That slithers into a wavering path
There is little traffic
But the stalks bend like they have a bad back

When night descends the near-deserted pasture
An eerie remnant remains in the air
Weighing it down
The desert-ness is like a scene from Murder Mystery
A sign with a cold steel handle reads
"Prison area. Do not pick up hitchhikers."
The stalks suspiciously stare at every passing car
Seeming to hide what might have happened

Don't dare look out the window
Past the rusted, bent chicken wire
For you might see a black plastic garbage bag

With a suspicious shape

When traveling amongst the dried grains
As the tall stalks loosely lean
Tauntingly teasing a tiresome driver
As the dangerously sweet wind decorates the heavy air
A driver can only intensely stare at the bright green stoplight ahead

Honesty

When the clouds roll in and the rain comes down
And the things I have on my mind get misty
All I want to do is rest in your arms
When the thunder is rumbling
And the lightning starts striking
All I want to do is hide in your Presence
When the flowers start wilting
And the floods start flowing
All I want to do is cower in your eyes
When the wind is blowing hard
And the crashing is too loud
All I want to do is sink into your shadow
When the grass can't even face it
And the trees are crying out
All we want to do is be with you

Icy Chills

Icy chills
But frightening thrills
As the cold-tipped will
Relies on nill
Reason fleeting
Conscience meeting
Never seeking
Someone weeping
Searching high
Full of lies
Then a faint cry
As people ask why
Understanding nothing
Creating something
Reaching for anything
A faint beat of the wings
Drowning in sorrow
Delving in sadness
Dipping in sulking
Drying out souls
Tip-toeing lines
Tight-rope decisions
Taunt guidelines
On the wrong side

Emotion Dance

Using pen to read emotion
When my honed-in meter is done
Not really happy or sad
Stuck in the in-between, bland
Not really sure what I want
Threads on my heart taunt
Know I should feel elated
Yet emotions still gated
Intensity abated
Stretch marks on my soul
Always telling, secrets sold
Maybe I have never been that bold
A muse for sadness
While my life doesn't mix
So I guess I hang in the balance
One step behind in this wary dance

Checkmate

I don't understand life
Why it exists
Why we need to live
I see humans and we look like pawns in a chess game
Being played by the earth
Every breath I take
Is checkmate
And I'm on the losing side
I am under attack
I cannot hide or run for shelter
I am stuck in the danger
Sacrificed to save those more important
Pieces move around me
Being played by a different hand
I stay rooted in my space
A circle trying to fit into a square
I hear the clinking of the marble
Feel the ground shift below
And yet as I sit and breathe
I am
Checkmate

Sometimes I Wonder

Sometimes I wonder if I was meant to be
When the trees are blowing
And the wind is howling
And the world is spinning

Sometimes I wonder if I was meant to see
When the ground is cracking
And the thunder's sounding
And the clouds are coming

Sometimes I wonder if I was meant to stay
When the time is nearing
And the voices I keep hearing
And the letters I keep writing

Sometimes I wonder if I was meant to cry
When nothing is freeing
And love is never nearing
And trust is always depleting

It Is

It is the fog folding over every inch, finger finding fallen foe
It is the dark, dreary shadow ducking into every corner
It is the heavy, hampered haze hanging in the balance
It is the milky, musty mist weeping in the muddled space
It is the tantalizing trance tripping tightwires
It is the ghostly, gathering gloom slumping over solidarity
It is neither black nor white, all or nothing
It is the gray, the steely middle, muted, murky
It is neither here nor there, present or past
It is the minute before and the eternity before that
It is the foreboding foreshadow of what is to come
It is the silky, shifty thoughts slipping through your fingers
It is intangible yet right within reach, just a moment too late
It is covert, cunning waiting for a clandestine encounter

It is overwhelming and obvious while being elusively endearing
It is the dark and the storm and the sky and the thunder
It is all that weighs down and that which lingers
It is

Seeking an End

Fluid Motion, tears in streams
It's not as hard as it may seem
Though once so brave, a warrior
Now wishes to be death's courier
The constant battle, constant war
And yet I know I have been here before
It comes too easy, have I come too far?
Yet all that life has set the bar
Wanting resistance
Experiencing surrender
Hating complacency
Bound to replication
Relief of stagnation
How far will this go?
When will it come, rock-bottom seeking
Not even sure anymore what's the meaning
Can teach the skills, I do that well
Yet cannot apply when the clouds befell
Future grim, sick of fighting
Because, man, these damn thoughts are biting
Exhausted from fighting, want it to end
Tired of making the truth bend

Never as it Seems

I am trying to figure out how it might be
That I feel more lonely with you
Then when it's just me
I sit here on edge always
With you right there
The awkwardness almost too much to bear
This is so confusing to me
I just can't seem to understand
And know you will never see
The nights when I am by myself
I find refuge, I can breathe
Thins with you that are just not felt
So many years we have been through
How can my comfort be at this level
And I know it's nothing new
Awareness is good for me
Or at least that's what I say out loud
Though my soul longs to just "be"
What do I deserve
What is my end game here
These convos in my head striking a nerve
Vacillating between numb and lonely and sorrow
I find myself lost
Here riding on time that is borrowed
I am not sure what that all means

Judgment weighs heavy
It's never as it seems

Ode to Staying Alive

An ode to those in that place
Blade in one hand, heart in the other
Tears even fear the darkness of that moment
Reason escapes, yet decisions have to be made
An ode to those that know the feeling well
That familiar yearn to escape, pain eluding
Breathing shallow, on the edge of control and powerlessness
Surge of adrenaline that makes you briefly reconsider
An ode to those with toes over the edge
Frantically trying to weigh the odds
Last-minute heart on the line
Where what you want feels so mixed up, an illusion
An ode to those whose blood is shaking
Everything from the inside out a bolt of electricity
Awareness all too keen- yet still feel unseen
At that moment in time finality seeming impossible
An ode to those
Those that choose to stay alive
Despite it all
Choice is made

Zingers

This tingle through my body
A twinge; long-lasting
Starting small; washing over me
No rhyme or reason
Shock by default
No strength left to shun
Head back, I let it wash over
Electricity spreading
Endpoint always unsure
Settling into my heart
A lightning bolt, jolt
Feeling pulled completely pulled apart
It settles to an ever-present ache
Throbbing, steady, pain
While I sit questioning why I'm still awake
Triggers are a mystery at times
Electricity not needing a reason
As I sit to myself, hanging on these lies
Hope I preach from my crumbling pedestal
Internal laughing, knowing all too well
That this game I try to sell
Reality hasn't yet had time to quell
Still I sit, jolted and silent
Emotions, body, mind just spent

End is Coming

The wind is breathing
The thunder beating
My brain and heart steeping
The longer it sits
The darker my thoughts get
Future unaccounted for
Fabric of security torn
Insecure and wary
Heartbeat blaring
Pelted by doubt
Love's ever-scorched drought
Yet pen flows freely
Even if their eyes don't see
The heart that shatters
Like it really even matters
Support runs dry
Even as I sit and cry
Tears ignored for too long
Are we just too far gone
Unending anguish
Spirits unable to lift
The pain intensifies
As the smile continues to lie
Kernel of truth
Sprouts from the ending of youth

Too old to correct
Too young to expect
Yet fear has its grip
Anxiety whips
Scars start to grow
Deeper than you'll ever know
Yet your care is lacking
Even as options start stacking
Ambivalence or ignorance?
Certainly not bliss
Feel the end coming
And that heartbeat keeps drumming
Quick and painless, hope declares
Yet destined for anguish, I despair

Disillusionment

The rain pelts the sidewalk around me
And my umbrella is punctured with holes
Puddles rise up around me
While my shoes soak through, penetrating my last layer of protection
I wish I would melt
Dissolve into the drops around me
I have never been that lucky
The wet is persistent and despite it, I feel parched
Soaked to the bone but hollow and dry to my soul
Precipitation pummeling the cage around my heart
Nothing has ever been able to get that close
The damp seeps up my legs, a slow crawl to soaking
Submerged standing on the cement
Still as an ever-changing statue
I am dripping but no emotions escape
I stare into the sheets, vacantly wandering into the unknown
I am particularly morose, with no protection in sight
So I stand and wish for it to wash me away
A portrait of disillusionment

Melt Away

I woke up this morning with sadness on my mind
The urge to cry but no tears to shed
The heartbeat ache for something more
While you lay in peace, dream in your slumber
I am plagued with the tornado of thoughts, sinking me slowly
Emotions are vague, blurred at the edges
Something so there, I know it, but cannot quite grasp
That is the way everything feels these days
Hollow expressions and tightrope conversations
It is lonely to be on this ship at night
No crews, no companions, just the darkness as a blanket
Not even the stars dare comfort
When I reach out my hand, everything is just too far
Like running in a dream but you don't actually move
Urgency courses through my blood
Yet there is nowhere for it to go, nothing to bind to
I wait for the rush, the molecules to push me forward

But my body is encased in amber
One day maybe beautiful, but now it is my living coffin
The world feels like an echo, sound but not quite real
Yet you stay in peaceful slumber
While I, the wet piece of paper, slowly melt away

How Do You Explain It

How do you explain it?
When the idea of it is drowned out by the tip-tap
Of the pelting rain on the windowsill of your soul
How do you explain it?
When it feels more like a fairytale
Then something that has ever existed
To you now or in the past
Where time feels muddled and pressed
Immeasurable and altogether consuming
How do you explain it?
This idea that is the foulest of "f words"
To those who have only seen the dark steps leading down
Light only in brief moments to their feet
Shoelace reflecting back only what they can immediately see
How do you explain it?
When any idea of possibilities
Has been so out of reach
It might as well be like jumping from star to star
On a beam of pure sadness
How do you explain it?
How do you say that any idea of a "future"

Is so foreign you aren't even sure what that means
How every moment of you fight your way
Hoping to convince it there will be another moment after
How just the mere ability
To eventually settle the debate with yourself
That there will be another moment
At times gets pulled out with the tide
And you have to search the shores once again
For evidence of breath, life, hope
So how do you explain it?
How do you say that when ending it all is only one moment away
A future beyond must have a hefty price
How do you explain how every moment is so hard
That a future seems overwhelming
Like building a wall that will fall on you
Crushing you and any moments you worked so hard to believe in
How do you explain it?

Tighten Your Grip

Tighten your grip
While I smile back
A tear may fall without permission
But I will not allow you to see my struggle
You will see the marks you left behind
In the vacancy of my eyes
But you will never see the scars on my mind
Fingerprints left on the dark recesses of my thoughts
You think you hurt me then
You think you hurt me now
But you will never know
How my calluses befriend your actions
How every time you squeeze a little tighter
My breath almost laughs
You think there is anything left of us to extinguish?
You don't see that I am already gone
So far that you can continue to pummel
And I won't feel a thing
So continue to tighten your grip
Squeeze a little harder
Watch the life fade
And watch me smile back
Knowing there was no life there anyway

This Fog

It's like a fog
Not the kind where you wake up and look out your window
Surprised by the misty welcoming and mysterious underpinnings
No, more like a gradual overtaking
When the storm clouds seem so distant
And you watch them come in
And gradually find yourself in the midst of the thunder and lighting
Wondering how that happened when you were JUST watching it
Or the smoke slowly rising from a charred earth
Until you're surrounded in white and it becomes your reality
This fog settles, heavy and consuming
Altering perspectives until it's all you know
This fog makes you forget what it was to see the picture clearly
Without the constant haze of the cloudy commitment
This fog convinces you it has always been this dense, this opaque, this burdensome
This fog convinces you that you should have always been that way

Stacked with all the burdens and guilt and truths
You try to bear every moment of every day
This fog whispers that it will always be there
Until you are convinced that this fog isn't the
reason you have trouble seeing
But the only reason you can see at all
Yes this fog breathes life and suffocation
Into every wary bit of your lasting soul
This fog
This slow-moving
Wrap around you
Hug while slowly taking every piece of you
This fog

Dimming of the Stars

There is some dimming in the stars I see
Quietly falling to earth
Sparkle of light drifting down
Away from the black-drawn night
Into the air of life-breathed dumb
Now onto the ground slowly numb
Quietly creeping up through the door
No need for knocking twice
Into the room of sleeping beds
Into the minds of quiet heads
Putting that twinkle in their eyes
Making a sparkle in the night
The sky is sad now, see it cry
For its glow is gone to use below
The moon has more craters now
As pieces provide the flick of light
To new voices, the sparkle goes
Our mind's fault
That there is a dimming in the stars I see

Printed in the USA
CPSIA information can be obtained
at www.ICGtesting.com
LVHW020519190524
780579LV00015B/903